make

1-hour gifts

16 Cheerful Projects to Sew

C&T PUBLISHING

Text, photography, and artwork copyright © 2017 by C&T Publishing, Inc.

Publisher: Amy Marson

Creative Director: Gailen Runge

Project Editor: Alice Mace Nakanishi

Compiler: Lindsay Conner

Cover/Book Designer: April Mostek

Page Layout Artist: Casey Dukes

Production Coordinator: Joe Edge

Photography by Nissa Brehmer, Christina Carty-Francis, and Diane Pedersen of C&T Publishing, Inc., unless otherwise noted

For further information and similar projects, see the book listed after each artist's bio.

Published by C&T Publishing, Inc., P.O. Box 1456, Lafayette, CA 94549

Contents

Baby Bib
Abbey Lane Quilts

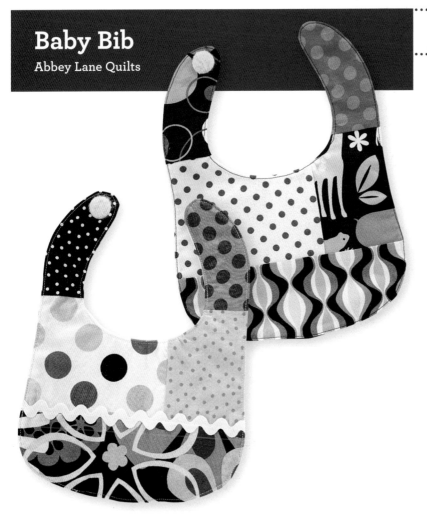

You can never have too many bibs for a baby. Grab some cute scraps for this quick and easy project and make a bib to match every outfit.

ABBEY LANE QUILTS is a pattern design company founded in 2008 by the team of Marcea Owen and Janice Liljenquist. Marcea is an entrepreneur and writer with a background in art and interior design. Janice is an accomplished quilting teacher and longarm quilter. Abbey Lane Quilts is based in Oviedo, Florida.

WEBSITE: abbeylanequilts.com

This project originally appeared in *Baby Times*, by Abbey Lane Quilts, available from Stash Books.

Materials and Cutting

Prewash all fabrics and canvas before cutting.

Materials	For	Cutting
Fabric A scrap		Cut 1 rectangle 5½″ × 4½″.
Fabric B scrap		Cut 1 rectangle 5½″ × 6½″.
Fabric C scrap	Bib front	Cut 1 rectangle 6½″ × 4½″.
Fabric D scrap		Cut 1 square 4½″ × 4½″.
Fabric E scrap		Cut 1 rectangle 3½″ × 10½″.
Fat quarter	Bib back	Cut 1 square 12½″ × 10½″.
Canvas: ⅜ yard	Bib lining	Cut 1 square 12½″ × 10½″.

Notions: ¾″ hook-and-loop dot, 11″ rickrack (*optional*), chalk or erasable marker

Instructions

1. Sew Fabric A to Fabric B along the 5½″ side. Press seam. This will be Row 1.

2. Sew Fabric C to Fabric D along the 4½″ side. Press seam. This will be Row 2.

3. Sew Rows 1 and 2 together. Press seam.

4. Sew Fabric E to the bottom of the unit. Press seam.

5. Make 2 copies of the Baby Bib pattern (page 46). Cut out the 2 pieces, flip one over, and tape them together along the dotted lines.

6. Layer the 3 fabric pieces in the following order:

- Canvas square on the bottom
- Backing square (right side up) in the middle
- Pieced top (wrong side up) on the top

7. Place the bib template on top of the stack and trace the outline with chalk or an erasable marker.

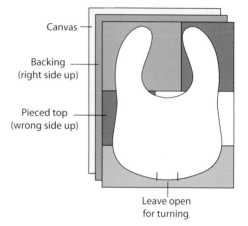

8. Pin all 3 layers together. Cut out the bib.

9. Sew around the entire bib, leaving a 2″ opening at the bottom. Clip the curves. Turn right side out and press.

10. Turn the opening in and pin closed. Topstitch around the entire bib. The top stitching will close the opening.

11. Sew one side of the hook-and-loop dot to each tab. One side will be on the front of the tab and the other will be on the back of the other tab.

tip It is helpful to sew the hook side of the dot on the back of the top tab and the soft loop side on the front of the bottom tab. This way the baby's hair is not so easily caught in the hook side of the dot.

Craft Apron

Virginia Lindsay

FINISHED SIZE: 17″ × 11″

When I have a booth at a craft show, I look forward to the time when I can walk around and shop the other tables. I started making these craft aprons to sell to other vendors and the many DIYers who are shopping. This design has seven pockets to keep you extra organized.

VIRGINIA LINDSAY is a self-taught sewist and lover of all things fabric. She is the author of a popular sewing blog and the designer behind Gingercake Patterns. Several of her patterns are published by Simplicity. Virginia lives in Freeport, Pennsylvania.

WEBSITE: gingercake.org

This project originally appeared in *Sewing to Sell—The Beginner's Guide to Starting a Craft Business*, by Virginia Lindsay, available from Stash Books.

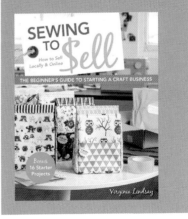

Fabric: Painter's drop cloth canvas, Kona Cotton in Tangerine from Robert Kaufman Fabrics, and Dolce by Tanya Whelan for FreeSpirit Fabric

Materials

Quilting-weight fabric is recommended for the pockets and works with a layer of fusible interfacing for the apron body. A heavier-weight fabric would also work for the apron body and eliminate the need for interfacing.

Cotton fabric

APRON BODY: 2 pieces 12″ × 18″

LARGE POCKET: 1 piece 14″ × 18″

SMALL POCKET: 1 piece 10″ × 18″

TIES: 2 pieces 3″ × 36″

Other

FUSIBLE INTERFACING: 1 piece 12″ × 18″ for apron body (needed if using quilting-weight cotton)

AIR- OR WATER-SOLUBLE FABRIC-MARKING PEN

LIGHTWEIGHT DOUBLE-SIDED FUSIBLE WEB (*optional*): Small scrap

Instructions

Seam allowances are ¼″ unless otherwise noted.

PREPARE THE PIECES

1. If you are using quilting-weight cotton for the main piece of the apron, follow the manufacturer's instructions to fuse interfacing to the wrong side of the 12″ × 18″ front apron body.

2. Fold the large pocket in half lengthwise, wrong sides together, to make a folded piece 7″ × 18″. Press the folded edge, pin if needed, and edgestitch along the fold.

3. Repeat Step 2 to fold, press, and stitch the smaller pocket to make a folded piece 5″ × 18″.

4. Test your fabric-marking pen on a scrap of your fabric and make sure the marks will come off easily. Use a ruler to mark the large pocket with a vertical line 6″ in from each end to make 3 even sections.

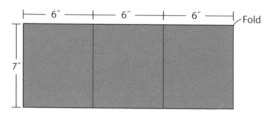

5. On the small pocket, mark a vertical line at the center (9″) and a line 4½″ on either side of the center to divide the pocket into 4 equal parts.

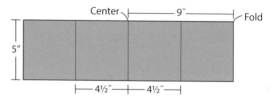

SEW THE DIVIDED POCKETS

1. Layer the small pocket on top of the large pocket, aligning the raw edges at the bottom. Sew through both pockets on the marked center line of the small pocket.

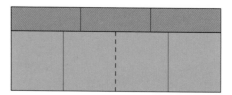

2. Layer the pocket unit on top of the front apron body piece, aligning the raw edges at the bottom. Fold (and pin if needed) the small pocket over to the center to expose the 6″ line on the large pocket underneath. Sew on the 6″ line through only the large pocket and the apron body.

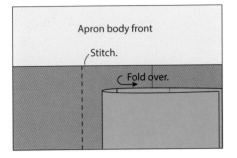

3. Unfold the small pocket to cover up the line you just sewed. Fold the apron body under toward the center. Sew through just the small and large pockets on the 4½″ line on the small pocket.

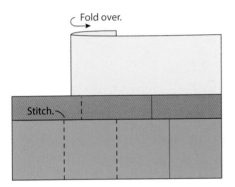

4. Repeat Steps 2 and 3 to sew the pockets on the other side of the apron. All this switching up of layers will give you 7 useful and different-sized pockets.

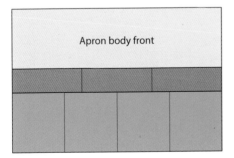

MAKE THE TIES

1. Fold and press the tie strips in half lengthwise, wrong sides together, and then fold and press the raw edges in toward the center fold. Edgestitch both ties closed along the open edges.

2. Pin the ties to the sides of the front apron body ¾″ down from the top edge. Baste in place. Knot the loose ends of the ties together in the center of the apron body and pin them down so they won't work their way back to the edge of the apron body for the next step.

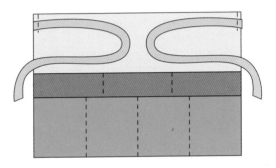

FINISH THE APRON

1. Pin both apron bodies right sides together, starting at the corners. Sew them together with a ½″ seam allowance, leaving a 4″–5″ opening on the top edge.

2. Trim the seams down to ¼″ and clip the corners. Pull the apron right side out through the opening. Poke out the corners with a chopstick, and iron the apron nice and flat. Fold the opening edges in and iron them flat so they match the seam.

3. I like to use a strip of fusible web to close up the opening. This will ensure that the opening looks nice and neat and is practically unnoticeable. Measure the opening and cut a piece of fusible web to fit. Fuse in place according to directions on the package.

If you prefer, blindstitch the opening closed.

4. Finally, edgestitch all the way around the apron to finish it up.

Fabric Bucket
Abbey Lane Quilts

ABBEY LANE QUILTS is a pattern design company founded in 2008 by the team of Marcea Owen and Janice Liljenquist. Marcea is an entrepreneur and writer with a background in art and interior design. Janice is an accomplished quilting teacher and longarm quilter. Abbey Lane Quilts is based in Oviedo, Florida.

WEBSITE: abbeylanequilts.com

This project originally appeared in *Baby Times*, by Abbey Lane Quilts, available from Stash Books.

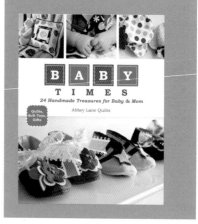

Materials and Cutting

Prewashing fabrics before cutting is optional for this project.

Materials	For	Cutting
Fabric A: ⅝ yard	Outer bucket	Cut 1 rectangle 18″ × 40″.
Fabric B: ⅞ yard	Inner bucket	Cut 1 rectangle 23¾″ × 40″.
	Handles	Cut 2 rectangles 3½″ × 8″.
Heavy-duty fusible interfacing (such as fast2fuse by C&T Publishing): 2⅜ yards	Outer interfacing	Cut 1 rectangle 18″ × 40″.
	Inner interfacing	Cut 1 rectangle 17¾″ × 40″.
	Handle interfacing	Cut 2 rectangles 1¼″ × 5⅞″.
Template material or stiff paper	Corner pattern	Cut 1 square 4½″ × 4½″.
Notions: Chalk or erasable marker		

Instructions

HANDLES

1. Fold over ¼" to the wrong side on each long side of the handle and press.

2. With wrong sides together, fold the handle in half lengthwise and press. Open the handle so the wrong side is up. Line up the edge of the fusible interfacing handle with the center fold. The ends of the fusible interfacing should be 1" shorter on each end, and one long side of the interfacing will fit under the folded edge of the fabric. Fuse into place.

3. Fold in the extra 1" on each end of the fabric and press. Fold the handle in half over the interfacing along the center crease. Pin the folded edges together and topstitch on all 4 sides.

tip To get a more finished look, we added an additional ¼" top stitch to each handle.

4. Repeat Steps 1–3 to make the other handle.

OUTER BUCKET

1. Fuse the outer fusible interfacing rectangle to the wrong side of the Fabric A outer rectangle.

2. On the right-hand side of the fabric, mark 8¼" from the left side of the rectangle and 4" down from the top with chalk or an erasable marker. Measure over 4½" and make another mark. Repeat, measuring in from the right.

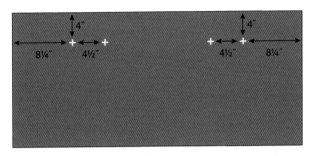

3. Line up the top corners of the handle with the marks. Stitch each end of the handle to the outside piece with 2 rows of top stitching.

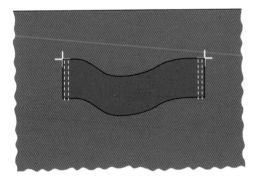

4. Fold the outer piece in half with right sides together and matching the short sides. Sew the 2 sides and the bottom of the outer piece together with a ¼" seam. Trim the seam allowances to ⅛". Place the outer piece on a flat surface with the side seam on the right and the folded edge on the left.

tip When you sew through fusible interfacing, sew each seam twice—the second seam directly on top of the first—to make the seam extra strong.

5. Line up the corner pattern with the seamlines on the bottom right side. Trace around the pattern. Line up the pattern with the fold line and bottom seamline on the left side. Trace around it.

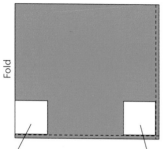
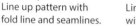

Line up pattern with fold line and seamlines.　　Line up pattern with seamlines.

6. Cut out the corners along the traced lines.

7. Bring the raw edges of each bottom cut-out square together, matching the bottom seam with the side seam on the right and with the fold line on the left. Pin and sew the raw edges together with a ¼" seam. Trim the seam allowance to ⅛".

8. Turn right side out. Press the side seams. Finger-press the bottom sides that aren't sewn so that they form a square.

INNER BUCKET

1. With the wrong side up, line up the inner fusible interfacing rectangle with 3 edges of the inner fabric rectangle. There will be an extra 6" of fabric on one short edge. Fuse the interfacing into place.

2. With right sides together, fold the inside piece in half and pin the short edges together. Make a mark on the top of the extra fabric ¼" from the raw edge. Make another mark ½" from the edge, right where the fusible interfacing starts. Draw a line to connect the 2 marks (see the diagram below).

3. With right sides still together, start at the top of the extra fabric and sew along the marked line. When you reach the fusible interfacing, continue sewing a ½" seam to the bottom. Trim the seam allowance to ⅛".

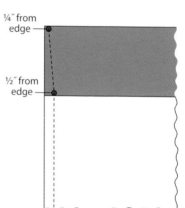

¼" from edge

½" from edge

4. Sew the bottom together with a ½" seam. Trim the seam allowance to ⅛".

5. Follow Outer Bucket, Steps 5–7 (page 9), to make the corners. Do not turn right side out.

6. Press the side seam. Finger-press the bottom sides that aren't sewn to form a square.

7. With wrong sides together, fold the extra fabric on the top in half and press the fold. The raw edge will be even with the fusible interfacing. Sew a double top stitch, ⅛" and ¼", around the folded edge.

8. Place the inner bucket into the outer bucket, making sure to line up the side seams. Push down the inner corners to make sure it is snug. The top edges of the fusible interfacing should be even on both pieces.

9. Fold the 3" band of fabric over the edge and down the outside of the bucket. Be sure to pull it all the way down.

Happiness Storage Tray

Annabel Wrigley

These cute-as-a-button trays are perfect for storing all your little treasures. Make a few to hold your favorite collections!

Fabric: Aviary by Joel Dewberry, Far Far Away II by Heather Ross

ANNABEL WRIGLEY is a crafty mom from Australia who now lives in the Virginia countryside. She owns Little Pincushion Studio, where she teaches girls everything they need to know to go forth and conquer the world of sewing and creating. She also shares her crafty ventures on Instagram.

WEBSITE: littlepincushionstudio.com

This project originally appeared in *We Love to Sew*, by Annabel Wrigley, available from FunStitch Studio.

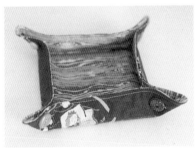

Project photos by Kristen Gardner

Materials

QUILTING-WEIGHT COTTON PRINT: 1 piece at least 10″ × 10″ for inside of tray

HEAVYWEIGHT COTTON PRINT: 1 piece at least 10″ × 10″ for outside of tray*

COTTON BATTING: 1 piece at least 10″ × 10″

BUTTONS: 8 assorted fun flat buttons with holes

SEWING MACHINE

BASIC SEWING SUPPLIES

* The heavier fabric on the outside helps make the tray nice and stiff.

Instructions

PREPARE THE PIECES

1. Cut a 9″ × 9″ square from each of the 2 fabrics. Cut a square from the batting, too.

2. Make a sandwich with the squares. Lay the batting on the bottom. Put the outside fabric square over it, right side facing up. Then put the inside fabric on top, with the right side down.

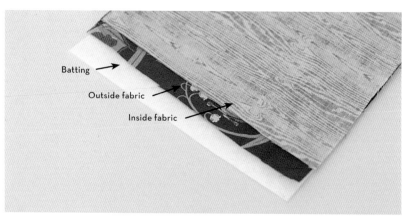

SEW THE TRAY

1. Make sure the pieces are lined up square. Pin around all 4 sides. (**Fig. A**)

2. Use the disappearing-ink marker to draw a 3″ line centered along one edge. (**Fig. B**)

3. Sew the pieces together. Sew with the edge of the presser foot on the edge of the fabric. Start at the top corner. Sew down to the bottom corner, and turn. Sew across the bottom to the beginning of the marked line. Start stitching again at the other end of the line; sew up the other side and around to the starting corner. Don't forget to backstitch at each start and stop! (**Fig. C**)

4. Sometimes the corners can seem a little bulky, so you may want to trim the corners. Do not cut into the stitching! Turn your tray right side out. The batting should be on the inside of the tray! (**Fig. D**)

5. Use the eraser end of a pencil to push out the corners so they are nice and neat. (**Fig. E**)

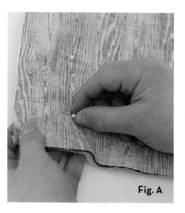

Fig. A

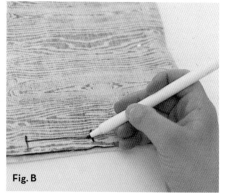

Fig. B

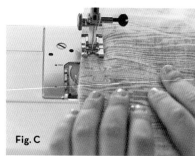

Fig. C

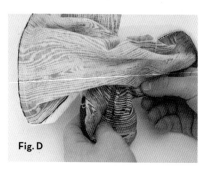

Fig. D

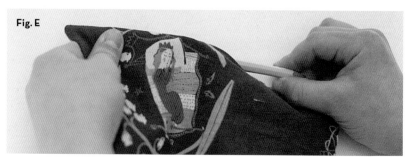

Fig. E

6. Time to turn on the iron. Carefully fold in the edges that are still open. Pin them in place. Iron the entire tray so it looks super neat and flat. (**Fig. F**)

Fig. F

Fig. G

7. Topstitch ¼" from the edge all the way around the square. This will make the edge look neat. It also closes up the opening in the edge of the square. (**Fig. G**)

8. Mark a 6" × 6" square exactly in the center of the square you have just sewn. Use your disappearing-ink marker. Hint: You can use a 6" square ruler as shown here. Or just measure with a regular ruler. (**Fig. H**)

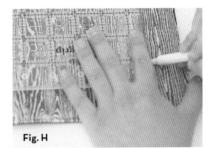
Fig. H

9. Before the disappearing ink actually disappears, sew around the square that you just marked. (**Fig. I**)

10. Using your disappearing-ink marker and a ruler, draw a line from a corner of the inner stitching to the corner of the square. This will be your guide for folding the corner. Repeat in the other 3 corners. (**Fig. J**)

Fig. I

11. Make a fold at a corner. (Look closely at the photo.) Make sure the top edges of the tray look even. Pin to hold the fold in place. Do this with all the corners. (**Fig. K**)

12. Imagine a line going from the bottom corner of the tray straight up. Find the halfway point, and mark it with a dot. This will be the button spot. (**Fig. L**)

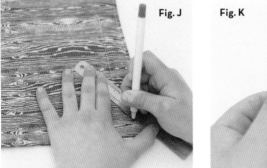
Fig. J

Fig. K

Fig. L

13. Use button thread in your needle. Push the needle and thread through one side of the folded corner, and then push it back through to the first side. Leave a nice long tail. Tie the tail and needle thread together with a knot. Be sure to pull tight to hold the corner together.

14. Now push your needle through the hole of a button, and sew back through the second hole to the other side of the corner. (**Fig. M**)

Fig. M

15. Now add another button to the other side of the corner. Go up through the first hole and then down through the remaining hole on that button and carefully back through to the side you started from. (**Fig. N**)

Fig. N

16. Tie a knot using the thread and the tail you left from the knot. Make sure to tie the knot behind the button and trim the thread so it doesn't show. It sounds complicated, but it really isn't! Be careful not to prick your fingers! Now do this with the remaining corners. (**Fig. O**)

Fig. O

Hipster Pocket Scarf

Lindsay Conner

This infinity-style scarf solves a common problem—what to do with your cash, cards, keys, or cell phone when you have no pockets and don't want to carry a purse. With your ID encased in the secure zippered pocket, you can leave your bulky bag at home!

LINDSAY CONNER is a writer, editor, and sewist. As a Craftsy blogger and Baby Lock designer, she designs patterns for books and magazines. The author of *Modern Bee—13 Quilts to Make with Friends*, Lindsay lives in Indianapolis, Indiana.

WEBSITES: lindsaysews.com, craftbuds.com

This project originally appeared in *On the Go Bags—15 Handmade Purses, Totes & Organizers,* by Lindsay Conner and Janelle MacKay, available from Stash Books.

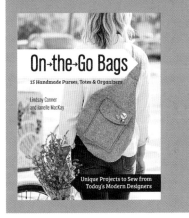

On-the-Go Bags

15 Handmade Purses, Totes & Organizers

Lindsay Conner and Janelle MacKay

Unique Projects to Sew from Today's Modern Designers

Fabric: Winged by Bonnie Christine for Art Gallery Fabrics

Materials

JERSEY KNIT FABRIC: ¾ yard, 58″ wide

ZIPPER: 7″ length, 1¼″ wide, heavy duty #5

STRETCH NEEDLE for sewing machine

Cutting

JERSEY KNIT FABRIC

Cut 1 piece 15″ × width of fabric for the scarf, making sure to find and cut with the grain.

Cut 1 piece 9″ × 15″ for the pocket (cutting the 9″ along the width of the fabric, parallel to the previous cut).

Cut 2 pieces 1½″ × 4″ for the zipper tabs.

NOTE: When cutting knit fabrics, it's important to cut along the straight grain so that your fabric hangs nicely and doesn't have any unusual twists. To find the natural grain of your knit, fold it in half crosswise, so the selvages are to the left and the right. Hold the cut raw edges of the fabric and let the bottom fold hang below. Gently shift the folded fabric until it hangs naturally—now you have found the grain. Pin along the fold and cut your pattern pieces accordingly. For example, if cutting a 15″ × width-of-fabric strip, cut 7½″ on each side of the pins.

Instructions

All seam allowances are ½″ unless otherwise noted.

SEW THE ZIPPERED POCKET

1. Fold a zipper tab in half crosswise. Unfold and fold the raw edges in to meet the center line. Repeat with the other zipper tab.

2. Sandwich the zipper tails on one end of the zipper between the layers of the folded zipper tab. Topstitch ³/16″ from the fold through all layers to secure the zipper end inside the tab. Make sure the zipper pull is out of the way when you sew. Repeat with the other end.

3. With the *right side* of the zipper facedown on the *right side* of the fabric, align a long edge of the zipper with a 9″ edge of the pocket. Stitch these together using a ¼″ seam allowance.

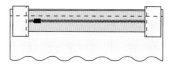

4. Fold the pocket over the seam and press.

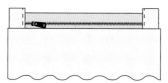

5. Repeat Steps 3 and 4 to stitch the other edge of the zipper to the other 9″ edge of the pocket, making a fabric loop.

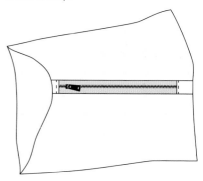

6. Topstitch both zipper seams ³/16″ from the edge, being careful not to stitch through the back of the pocket.

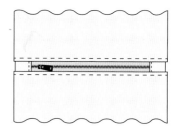

SEW THE SCARF

1. Fold the scarf in half lengthwise, right sides together, and pin the long raw edges together. Stitch along the seam you've pinned, leaving a 3″ section open in the center for turning. Press the seam of the long tube open.

2. With the scarf still turned *wrong side out*, insert the zippered pocket into one open end so that the right sides are together and the raw edges are aligned. The long scarf seam should run opposite the zipper, which is the front of the scarf. Pin the raw edges of the scarf to the pocket, easing the fabric as you go around the loop.

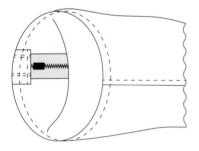

3. Stitch the pocket to the scarf by sewing around the loop to join both tubes.

4. Reach inside the tube to pull the other side of the pocket toward the other raw edges of the scarf. Align the raw edges, making sure that the scarf is not twisted and that the long scarf seam runs opposite the zipper. Pin the raw edges together and repeat Step 3.

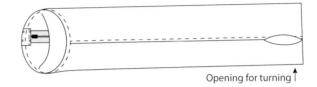

Opening for turning ↑

5. Reach inside the 3″ opening in the scarf and pull the scarf *right side out*. Position the seams on both ends of the pocket away from the zipper and press along the seams.

6. Stitch in-the-ditch along both seams joining the scarf to the pocket. Topstitch 3/16″ away from both seams on the scarf side of the pocket. Hand or machine stitch the opening closed.

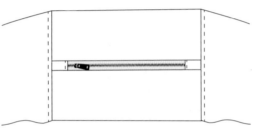

NOTE: The scarf may be doubled or tripled—either way, your valuables are encased in the roomy pocket and won't slide around in the body of the scarf.

Notepad Cover
Sweetwater

Remember those book covers we were required to slip on our junior high textbooks? Try this updated version! Two inside pockets hold two notepads 5″ × 8″; a magnetic closure keeps them secure.

Photo by Farmhouse Creations, Inc.

SWEETWATER was founded in 2001 by Karla Eisenach and her two daughters, Lisa Burnett and Susan Kendrick. Located in Colorado, Sweetwater's simple yet sophisticated aesthetic infuses their many product lines, including fabric and quilt patterns for Moda.

WEBSITE: thesweetwaterco.com

This project originally appeared in *Sweetwater's Simple Home*, by Sweetwater, available from Stash Books.

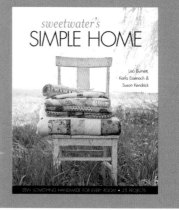

Materials

Makes 1 cover to hold 2 notepads.

OUTSIDE, LINING, AND CLOSURE TAB: ⅓ yard

POCKETS: ⅓ yard

COTTON BATTING: 14″ × 11″

IRON-ON FABRIC LABEL OR 1 SHEET OF IRON-ON INKJET-PRINTABLE FABRIC

½″ MAGNETIC SNAP

NOTEPADS: 2, sized 5″ × 8″

Instructions

Use the closure tab pattern (page 46); a ¼″ seam allowance is included.

OUTSIDE AND BATTING

1. Cut 1 piece 12½″ × 9½″ from the outside fabric.

2. With the right side up, center the outside piece over the cotton batting.

3. Baste the outside fabric and the cotton batting together, close to the raw edge.

4. Trim away the excess batting and treat the two pieces as one.

LABEL

1. To make the fabric labels using a computer and iron-on inkjet-printable fabric, follow the instructions of the printable-fabric manufacturer to make a label measuring 1″ × 3″.

2. Peel off the paper backing (if there is one) from the label and iron it to the center of the outside piece, with the label positioned vertically.

3. Stitch close around the edge of the label.

LINING AND POCKETS

1. Cut 1 piece 12½″ × 9½″ from the lining fabric.

2. Cut 1 pocket piece 12½″ × 12″ from the pocket fabric.

3. Fold the pocket piece in half with the wrong sides together, matching the 12½″ sides. Press.

4. Place the folded pocket piece over the lining piece, matching the raw edges at the sides and bottom.

5. Baste the pocket to the lining close to the raw edges.

6. Stitch down the center of the pocket to form 2 pockets, as shown.

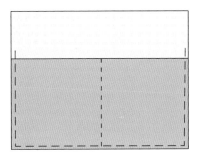

Baste pocket to lining.

Photo by Farmhouse Creations, Inc.

CLOSURE TAB

1. Use the pattern to cut 2 pieces for the tab. Cut a piece of batting 3½″ × 5″.

2. With right side up, center 1 tab piece over the cotton batting.

3. Baste the fabric and batting together, close to the raw edge. Trim away the excess batting. This will be the underside of the tab.

4. Apply 1 part of the magnetic closure to the underside of the tab according to the manufacturer's directions. Position the magnet closure in the center and ¾″ in from the edge.

5. With the right sides together, place the remaining tab piece over the underside piece. Sew the pieces together, leaving the straight side open.

6. Trim the seam allowance to ⅛″.

7. Turn the closure tab right side out and press.

8. Topstitch close to the edge.

9. Center the tab along the left 9½″ edge of the outside piece, with the underside facing up. Baste in place.

10. Apply the second part of the magnet closure to the opposite side on the outside cover, placing the closure in the center and 1″ in from the edge.

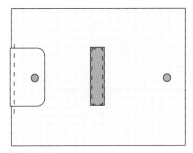

Baste tab to cover.

FINISHING

1. With the right sides together, pin the lining to the outside.

2. Trim all the corners to make them rounded.

3. Sew the lining and the outside cover together all around the edge, leaving a 3″ opening at the bottom.

4. Turn the piece right side out through the opening. Press.

5. Topstitch close to the edge around the entire cover. This will secure the opening closed.

6. Insert a notepad into each pocket.

Sunglasses Case

Sue Kim

How can you keep your sunglasses safe? Invest an hour and make a sunglasses case! You can use either home decorator or quilting-weight cotton fabric.

SUE KIM has been creating sought-after modern bag designs for many years. She started sewing when she was ten and always had a passion for crafts. An independent pattern designer, she is also a best-selling author and contributes to several pattern companies. She lives in Manitoba, Canada.

WEBSITE: suekimdesigns.com

This project originally appeared in *Bags—The Modern Classics*, by Sue Kim, available from Stash Books.

Materials

Fabric amounts are based on 44″-wide fabric.

EXTERIOR: ¼ yard

LINING: ¼ yard

FUSIBLE FLEECE INTERFACING:
³⁄₈ yard, 22″ wide

14 MM MAGNETIC SNAP

BUTTON: ³⁄₄″ diameter

Cutting

Use the Sunglasses Case patterns (page 47).

EXTERIOR
Cut 2 Front/Back pieces.

Cut 1 piece 7¹⁄₂″ × 4″ for the flap.*

LINING
Cut 2 Front/Back pieces.

Cut 1 piece 7¹⁄₂″ × 4″ for the flap.*

INTERFACING
Cut 2 Front/Back pieces.

Cut 1 piece 7¹⁄₂″ × 4″ for the flap.*

* Refer to the Flap diagram to mark the pieces and to trace and trim the bottom corners, using the Sunglasses Case Flap Corner pattern.

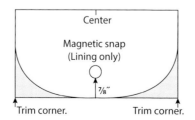

Center

Magnetic snap
(Lining only)

⁷⁄₈″

Trim corner.   Trim corner.

Flap

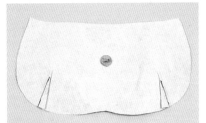

Fig. A Sew front darts, and press toward center.

Fig. B Sew back darts, and press toward outside edge.

Fig. C Sew side and bottom edges.

Fig. D Insert exterior inside lining.

Instructions

SEWING THE EXTERIOR AND LINING

1. Fuse the interfacing to the wrong side of the exterior pieces.

2. Attach the magnetic snap to the exterior front and on lining flap pieces as marked (see Adding a Magnetic Snap, page 22).

3. Sew the darts on the exterior front and back pieces and the lining front and back pieces. To sew the darts, transfer the A and B points from the pattern to the fabric. Fold the fabric, and match and pin the A points with right sides together. Sew the dart seam from points A to B, backtacking at both ends.

4. Press the darts on the front pieces toward the center. Press the darts on the back pieces toward the outside edge. (**Figs. A & B**)

5. Pin the front and back exterior pieces with the right sides together. The darts on the front and back pieces will be pressed in opposite directions, so they will lie flat.

6. Sew around the side and bottom edges, backtacking at each end. Notch the seam. (**Fig. C**)

7. Repeat Steps 5 and 6 for the lining.

8. Press the exterior and lining seams open. Turn the exterior right side out. Insert the exterior inside the lining, with right sides together. (**Fig. D**)

9. Pin the exterior and lining together around the top opening. (**Fig. E**)

10. Sew around the opening, leaving 3″ unstitched for turning. Trim the corners at the tops of the seams. Turn right side out. Tuck the lining into the exterior. Press the opening, including the seam allowances of the unstitched opening, and pin. (**Fig. F**)

11. Topstitch around the opening ⅛″ from the edge. The folded-in edges will be secured in the topstitching.

Fig. E Pin around top opening.

Fig. F Turn, press, and pin opening.

Adding a Magnetic Snap

You should attach the magnetic snap following the manufacturer's instructions, but here's how it is generally done:

1. Cut a piece of interfacing approximately 1½" × 1½". Center the interfacing over the marked snap position on the wrong side of the fabric and fuse it in position. Then center the metal support piece on top of the interfacing, over the marked snap position. (**Fig. A**)

2. Trace around the metal support piece, including the holes for the prongs. (**Fig. B**)

3. Carefully snip the holes for the prongs, through all the layers. (**Fig. C**)

4. From the right side of the fabric, insert the prongs of a magnetic snap piece. (**Fig. D**)

5. Place the metal support of the snap over the prongs. Fold the prongs away from the center over the disc. (**Fig. E**)

6. Repeat Steps 1–5 to attach the other half of the magnetic snap to the corresponding piece of fabric. (**Fig. F**)

Fig. A Position metal support over snap position.

Fig. B Trace metal support piece.

Fig. C Snip holes for prongs through all layers.

Fig. D Insert magnetic snap piece.

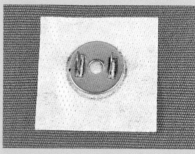
Fig. E Fold prongs away from center.

Fig. F Completed half of magnetic snap

Making the Flap

1. Pin the exterior flap and lining flap with right sides together. Stitch around the flap, leaving 3" unstitched on the top straight edge for turning. Trim the corners, and notch the curved seam. Trim the seam allowance to ¼".

2. Turn right side out. Press, and topstitch ⅛" from the curved seam only. Tuck in the seam allowances on the unstitched opening, press, and slipstitch the opening closed.

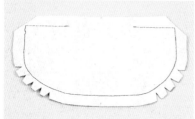
Stitch around flap, leaving 3" unstitched.

Topstitch curved seam only.

Finishing the Bag

1. Center the flap on the back of the exterior, with the straight edge along the flap stitching line, and pin in place. Check the position of the magnetic snap, and adjust the flap if needed.

2. Topstitch the flap in place, ⅛" from the straight edge, backtacking at both ends.

3. Sew the button to the exterior flap in the desired location.

Finished! Enjoy the sun!

Pin flap to back.

Sweet and Sour Apple Coasters
Kajsa Wikman

FINISHED SIZE: *4" × 4"*
(10.2 cm × 10.2 cm)

This set of four coasters is a sweet and fun project for when you don't have much time.

KAJSA WIKMAN is an artist, designer, and blogger. She also runs a business, Syko Design, which specializes in happy, child-like appliqué designs and printed products. Kajsa lives in Ekenäs, Finland.

WEBSITE: syko.fi

This project originally appeared in *Scandinavian Stitches*, by Kajsa Wikman, available from Stash Books.

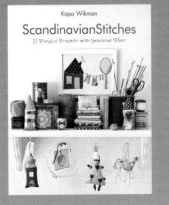

Materials

Fabrics

NATURAL-COLORED LINEN OR COTTON: ¼ yard (25 cm) for backgrounds and backing

RED: 3 squares 5″ × 5″ (13 cm × 13 cm) for apples

LIME GREEN: 1 square 5″ × 5″ (13 cm × 13 cm) for apples

WHITE AND BLACK SCRAPS: For apple cores and seeds

Notions

LOW-LOFT BATTING: ¼ yard (25 cm)

PAPER-BACKED FUSIBLE WEB: ¼ yard (25 cm)

THREADS:

Black machine embroidery thread (30-weight)

White machine quilting thread (30-weight)

Cutting

LINEN: Cut 8 squares 4½″ × 4½″ (11.4 cm × 11.4 cm).

BATTING: Cut 4 squares 4½″ × 4½″ (11.4 cm × 11.4 cm).

Instructions

Seam allowances are ¼″ (6 mm) unless otherwise noted.

1. Trace the appliqué patterns (page 47) onto the paper side of the fusible web. Roughly cut out the pieces with at least a ¼″ (6 mm) allowance. Place the pieces with the paper side up on the wrong side of the fabric, and press them using a dry iron. Peel off the paper on the back of the appliqué pieces. Position the pieces on 4 linen squares (see the project photo). Press.

2. Thread the sewing machine with black embroidery thread. Sew carefully with a short straight stitch around the edges of each apple, using the appliqué foot on your sewing machine. Stitch the core and the seeds. Then set the sewing machine for a short and wide zigzag stitch to make the stems. Try out the stitches on a scrap first to be sure to get the stems you want!

3. Thread the machine with regular sewing thread. Place the batting pieces under the apple squares. Pin the appliquéd linen squares and the linen backing squares right sides together, and stitch ¼″ (6 mm) from the edges, leaving an opening. Trim the corners. Turn the pieces right side out, and press.

4. Thread your sewing machine with white thread. Stitch close to the edges of the apples to quilt the coasters. Topstitch with a straight stitch using black thread close to the edges. This will close the openings.

Invite your friends to dinner!

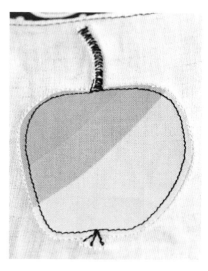

Tote Bag

Sara Trail

FINISHED SIZE: Approx. 15″ × 15″

Tote bags are all the rage and easy to make. Embellishments like patches, pins, or funky buttons can turn yours into something awesome!

SARA TRAIL wrote her first book, *Sew with Sara*, when she was only 13. Now a graduate of UC Berkeley and a student at the Harvard Graduate School, she owns and runs the Social Justice Sewing Academy, which empowers a new generation of leaders through sewing. Sara lives in Boston, Massachusetts.

WEBSITE: sjsacademy.com

This project originally appeared in *Sew with Sara* by Sara Trail, available from C&T Publishing.

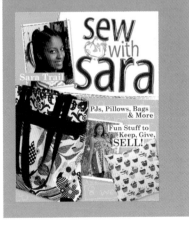

Materials

FABRIC A: ½ yard for main body

FABRIC B: ¼ yard for middle strip

FABRIC C: ¼ yard for top strip

LINING: ½ yard

STRAPS: ⅜ yard

FUSIBLE INTERFACING OR BATTING: 15½″ × 4½″

MATCHING THREAD

PARCHMENT PAPER OR APPLIQUÉ PRESSING SHEET

Cutting

FABRIC A: Cut 2 rectangles 12½″ × 15½″.

FABRIC B: Cut 2 strips 2½″ × 15½″.

FABRIC C: Cut 2 strips 3½″ × 15½″.

LINING: Cut 1 rectangle 15½″ × 34½″.

STRAPS: Cut 2 strips 5″ × width of fabric.

Instructions

1. Using a ¼″ seam allowance, sew each middle strip to a top strip along the long edge (15½″), right sides together. Press the seams open.

2. Line up a long edge (15½″) of each main body rectangle with a middle strip from the sewn sets from Step 1, right sides together. Pin and sew the pieces together. Press the seams open.

Sew a strip set to each main body piece.

3. Layer the 2 pieced panels, right sides together. Sew the panels together along the bottom edges of the main body rectangles. Press the seams open.

Sew the bottom edges together.

4. Protect your ironing surface with parchment paper or an appliqué pressing sheet. Place the pieced body panel *wrong* side up on the protected surface. Line up the fusible (shiny) side of the interfacing or batting with the wrong side of the body. Fuse the interfacing or batting, following the manufacturer's directions.

Fuse the interfacing to the wrong side of pieced body.

5. Layer the body and lining, *wrong* sides together, and line up the edges. The interfacing or batting will be sandwiched between the 2 fabric layers. Using a long basting stitch, sew around all the edges, ¼″ from the edge. If necessary, trim the edges even with the edges of the pieced body.

6. Fold the sandwiched layers together along the bottom seam, lining side out. Pin the sides together, making sure the side seams are lined up. Sew each side seam with a ¼″ seam allowance.

7. Fold the bottom corners, matching the side and bottom seams, to form a triangle. Pin in place. Measure and mark a line 2″ in from the triangle's point.

Fold the bottom corners to make a triangle.

8. Sew along the marked line at each corner, backstitching at each end, then trim the seam allowance to ¼″. Turn the bag right side out.

9. At the top opening of the tote, fold under ¼″ of the edge toward the lining side. Press in place. Then turn under another ½″ to make a hem. Press in place.

10. Use the strap fabric to make 2 straps. I usually make my straps 30″ long, but they can be as long or as short as you'd like. To make the straps, fold and press the fabric strip in half lengthwise, wrong sides together, to make a center crease.

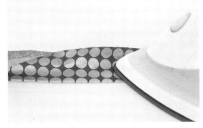

Fold the fabric strip wrong sides together.

11. Open up the fabric strip and lay it flat on your ironing surface. Fold a long edge in toward the center crease, wrong sides together, and press.

Fold one long edge toward the center crease.

12. Fold the other long edge in toward the center crease, wrong sides together, and press. You now have 2 folded edges, both meeting at the center crease.

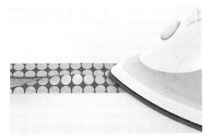

Both long edges are folded in toward the center crease.

13. Refold and press the fabric strip along the center crease, keeping the raw edges inside this fold. Once the strip is folded, you will *not* see the 2 long cut edges. Topstitch ¼″ away from the long open edge of the strap. Then topstitch ¼″ away from the other folded edge of the strap.

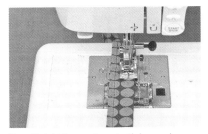

Topstitch ¼″ away from both long edges.

tip When you make the straps, you can add a strip of fusible interfacing or batting before you do the topstitching. The extra thickness will make the tote look more expensive.

14. Tuck the ends of each strap underneath the folded hem, 3″ in from each side seam. The straps will be facing down into the bag. Pin in place.

15. Sew around the entire opening, ¼″ from the bottom of the folded hem, remembering to backstitch when you start and stop sewing.

16. Fold the straps up and out of the bag, and pin in place. Secure the straps to the opening by sewing them ¼″ from the top edge of the bag. Backstitch to lock the stitches. Securing the straps reinforces them so the bag can carry more.

17. Press the tote and you are done!

Zippy Pouch

Annabel Wrigley

FINISHED SIZE: 8½″ × 6½″

You can never have enough bags! This little cutie is perfect for carrying everything you could possibly need.

Fabric: Birch Fabrics, Premier Prints

Project photos by Kristen Gardner

ANNABEL WRIGLEY is a crafty mom from Australia who now lives in the Virginia countryside. She owns Little Pincushion Studio, where she teaches girls everything they need to know to go forth and conquer the world of sewing and creating. She also shares her crafty ventures on Instagram.

WEBSITE: littlepincushionstudio.com

This project originally appeared in *We Love to Sew*, by Annabel Wrigley, available from FunStitch Studio.

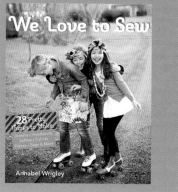

Materials

OUTSIDE: ¼ yard of fun printed fabric

LINING: ¼ yard

9″ ZIPPER

EMBROIDERY THREAD (*optional*): For zipper pull

YARN (*optional*): For zipper pull

SEWING MACHINE AND ZIPPER FOOT

BASIC SEWING SUPPLIES

Cutting

OUTSIDE: Cut 2 pieces 7″ × 9″.

LINING: Cut 2 pieces 7″ × 9″.

Instructions

1. Lay 1 lining piece and 1 outside bag piece *wrong* sides together and pin them in place. This picture shows the outside piece on top. (**Fig. A**)

2. Fold down both layers together ¼″ at the top edge. Fold them onto the lining side. (The photo shows the lining side.) Iron them flat. Do the same thing with the other 2 pieces. (**Fig. B**)

3. Lay the zipper right side up. (The right side of the zipper is the side with the zipper pull on it.) Lay the folded edge of 1 pouch piece, lining side down, over the fabric part of the zipper next to one side of the zipper teeth. (**Fig. C**)

4. Carefully pin the fabric piece to the zipper. (**Fig. D**)

5. Repeat Steps 3 and 4 with the other pouch piece. Pin this piece to the opposite side of the zipper teeth.

6. Now attach the zipper foot to your sewing machine. Attach the foot with the needle on the right-hand side so it will be close to the zipper teeth when you sew. (**Fig. E**)

7. Carefully sew all the way down both sides of the zipper, with the edge of the zipper foot butted up to the edge of the zipper teeth. When you are finished, change back to the regular presser foot. (**Fig. F**)

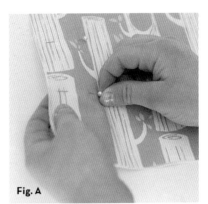

Fig. A

Fig. B

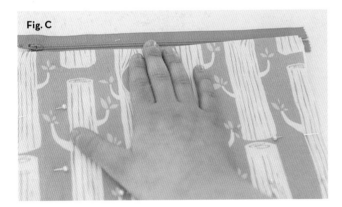

Fig. C

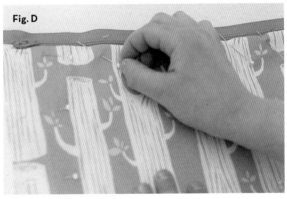

Fig. D

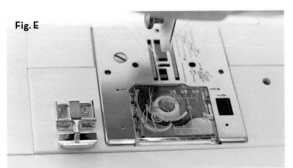

Fig. E

Fig. F

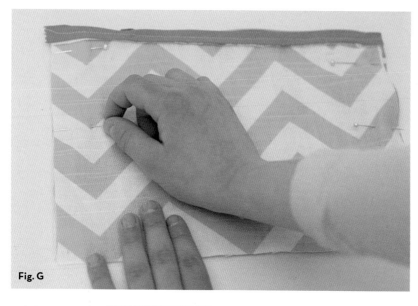

Fig. G

8. Unzip the zipper so you can turn it right side out later. Fold the pouch out so that the right sides are facing. Pin around the sides and bottom. (**Fig. G**)

9. Now sew all 3 sides with the edge of the presser foot on the edge of the fabric. Make sure to start and end with a backstitch. (**Fig. H**)

10. Trim the points off the corners. Don't cut into your stitching! Trim all those pesky threads. (**Fig. I**)

11. Turn the pouch right side out. You may want to iron it to make it look super sharp! (**Figs. J & K**)

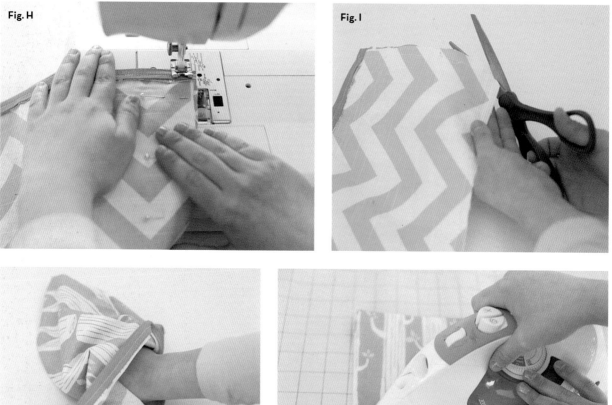

Fig. H

Fig. I

Fig. J

Fig. K

Drawstring Backpack

Virginia Lindsay

Anyone who can sew can make this bag easily. What's fun about the style of this little backpack is that it is full of potential for all sorts of bright prints and fun uses.

Fabric: Moxie by Erin McMorris for FreeSpirit Fabric

VIRGINIA LINDSAY is a self-taught sewist and lover of all things fabric. She is the author of a popular sewing blog and the designer behind Gingercake Patterns. Several of her patterns are published by Simplicity. Virginia lives in Freeport, Pennsylvania.

WEBSITE: gingercake.org

This project originally appeared in *Sewing to Sell—The Beginner's Guide to Starting a Craft Business*, by Virginia Lindsay, available from Stash Books.

Materials

Quilting-weight fabric is recommended.

EXTERIOR: 1 piece at least 14″ × 36″ of cotton fabric

LINING: 1 piece at least 14″ × 36″ of cotton fabric

RICKRACK OR ½″-WIDE RIBBON: 8″ length

NYLON CORDING: 4 yards, ⅛″ diameter

Instructions

Seam allowances are ¼" unless otherwise noted. Backstitch at the beginning and end of each seam.

MAKE THE EXTERIOR AND LINING

1. Cut both the exterior and lining fabrics into 2 pieces each (4 total) 14" × 18".

2. Cut the rickrack into 2 pieces 4" long. Fold the rickrack piece in half to make loops. Aligning the raw edges, pin each loop in place 1" up from the bottom of 1 exterior bag piece, right side up, as shown.

3. Pin both exterior bag pieces, right sides together, with the loops sandwiched in between. Mark 2" down from the top in the seam allowance on the wrong side of 1 bag piece. Starting at the mark, sew down one long 18" side, pivot and stitch across the bottom, and pivot and stitch up the other long side, stopping at the other mark 2" from the top edge.

4. Clip the corners. Clip **to**, *but not through*, the side seam allowances where seams begin and end. Turn the bag exterior right side out. Press.

5. Repeat Steps 3 and 4 with the lining pieces, but make sure to *leave a 4" gap* at the bottom of the lining so you can turn the bag right side out later. Do *not* clip the seam allowances.

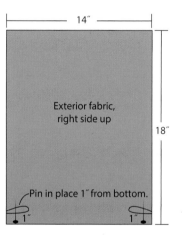

14"

Exterior fabric, right side up

18"

Pin in place 1" from bottom.

1" 1"

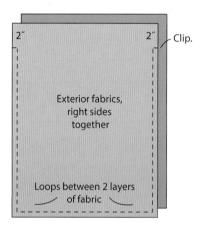

2" 2" — Clip.

Exterior fabrics, right sides together

Loops between 2 layers of fabric

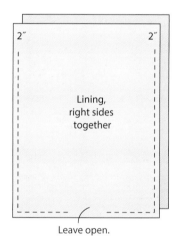

2" 2"

Lining, right sides together

Leave open.

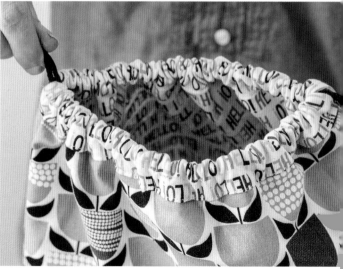

6. Insert the bag exterior into the bag lining, right sides together, and line up the upper raw edges and the side seams.

7. On one side of the bag *only*, pin the lining and exterior pieces together along the upper edge of the bag and down the open 2″ where the side seam stopped. Flip the exterior seam allowances out at the clip to meet the raw edges of the lining.

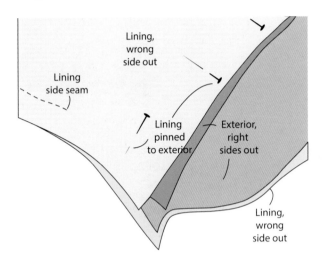

8. Starting where the side seam stopped and making sure to backstitch or lock your stitches, continue sewing up the open side (this time through 1 lining and 1 exterior piece instead of both exterior pieces or both lining pieces). Pivot at the corner, stitch across the upper edge, pivot at the opposite corner, and stitch down the side, stopping and backstitching at the opposite side seam.

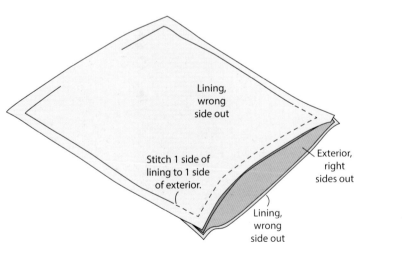

9. Repeat Steps 7 and 8 on the opposite side of the bag with the remaining open lining and exterior edges.

10. Turn the bag right side out through the opening in the lining. Push the lining inside the exterior. Reach through the opening in the lining and poke out the exterior corners with a chopstick. Pull the lining back out and press the raw edges of the opening inside. Sew the opening closed, either by hand with a blind stitch or by machine with an edge stitch, as close to the edge as possible. Push the lining back inside the bag a final time and press the upper edge of the bag nice and flat.

MAKE THE CASING

1. Fold the upper edge of the bag down 1″ to the outside and press flat. Pin all around the bag and sew the folded edge down about ⅛″ from the seam. If your machine has a free arm, use it to make it easier to sew all around.

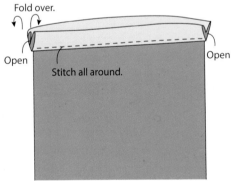

2. Cut the cording into 2 equal lengths.

3. Use a safety pin or bodkin at one end of a piece of cord to thread it through one side of the casing. When you get to the opening on the other side, continue through the other side until you are back where you began. Take off the safety pin and gently pull the cord through the casing (without drawing up the casing) so that both ends are even. Thread one of the ends through the loop at the bottom of the bag and then tie the ends together in a tight knot. Apply Fray Check to the cut ends, if you like.

4. Repeat Step 3 with the other piece of cord, starting at the opposite end of the casing.

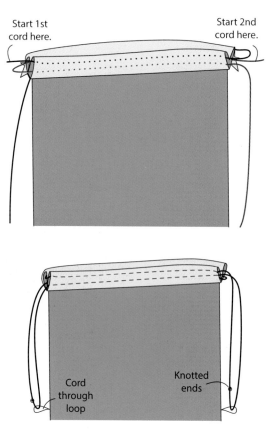

5. *Optional:* To add a little more structure to the bag, poke out the bottom corners of the bag, line up the bottom and side seams, and flatten the corner into a triangle shape. Pin flat and mark a line with chalk or removable ink 1½" from the tip of the corner. Sew on the line, making sure not to catch the loop or drawstring.

6. Pull the drawstring cords from opposite ends and gather the casing to make a stylish and functional backpack that you will love.

Suggestions

- Add a pocket for a fun and easy addition to the front or sides of the backpack.

- Experiment with different types of fabric and patchwork, but don't get too bulky because the drawstring won't work as easily with thick fabrics.

Easy Lazy Bag

Sue Kim

FINISHED SIZE: approx.
14″ × 14″, plus 10″ handles (tied)

Do you have those days when you want to sew but you don't have a lot of time? Then this is the bag for you. It's the perfect lazy Saturday afternoon project! You can use either home decorator or quilting-weight cotton fabric.

SUE KIM has been creating sought-after modern bag designs for many years. She started sewing when she was ten and always had a passion for crafts. An independent pattern designer, she is also a best-selling author and contributes to several pattern companies. She lives in Manitoba, Canada.

WEBSITE: suekimdesigns.com

This project originally appeared in *Bags—The Modern Classics*, by Sue Kim, available from Stash Books.

Materials

Fabric amounts are based on 44″-wide fabric.

EXTERIOR: 1 yard

LINING: 1 yard

LIGHTWEIGHT FUSIBLE INTERFACING (*optional*): 1¾ yards, 22″ wide

18 MM MAGNETIC SNAP

HOOK-AND-LOOP TAPE: 4″–5″ for pocket closure

Cutting

Use the Easy Lazy Bag Front/Back: 1 and the Easy Lazy Bag Front/Back: 2 patterns (page 48). Join them together as indicated to make one pattern piece.

EXTERIOR
Cut 2 Front/Back pieces.

LINING
Cut 2 Front/Back pieces.

Cut 2 pieces 7″ × 7″ for the pocket.

INTERFACING
Cut 2 Front/Back pieces.

Instructions

MAKING THE POCKET

1. Center 1 piece of hook-and-loop tape on the right side of a pocket fabric piece, with the top edge of the tape 1″ from the top edge of the fabric. Sew around all 4 edges, backtacking at the starting and ending points. This will become the lining side of the pocket. (**Fig. A**)

2. Pin the pocket pieces together with right sides facing. Sew around all 4 sides using a ½″ seam allowance, leaving 4″ unstitched along the top edge (nearest the hook-and-loop tape) for turning. Trim the corners. (**Fig. B**)

3. Turn the pocket right side out, and use a sharp tool to carefully push the corners out. Fold the raw edges of the opening to the inside, and press the pocket. Pin the opening. From the exterior side, topstitch the top edge ⅛″ from the edge, backtacking at both ends. The folded-in edges will be secured in the topstitching. (**Fig. C**)

4. Center the pocket on the right side of a lining front or back piece, with the lower edge of the pocket placed 3½″ from the bottom edge of the lining. After stitching in place the other piece of hook-and-loop tape on the right side of the corresponding bag lining, topstitch the pocket in place on top of it—down one side, across the bottom, and back up the other side, backtacking at both ends.

SEWING THE EXTERIOR AND LINING

1. If you choose to use interfacing, fuse it to the wrong side of the exterior front and back pieces.

2. Pin the exterior front and back pieces around the side and bottom edges, with right sides together. (**Fig. D**)

3. Sew around the side and bottom edges, backtacking at both ends. Notch the rounded corner seams.

4. Attach the magnetic snap to the lining front and back pieces as indicated on the pattern (see Adding a Magnetic Snap, page 22).

5. Repeat Steps 2 and 3 with the lining front and back pieces, leaving 5″ unstitched along the bottom edge for turning.

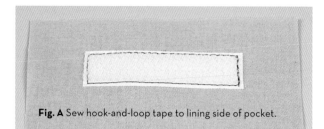

Fig. A Sew hook-and-loop tape to lining side of pocket.

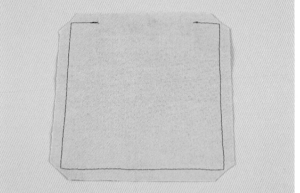

Fig. B Sew pocket, leaving opening for turning.

Fig. C Topstitch along top edge from exterior side.

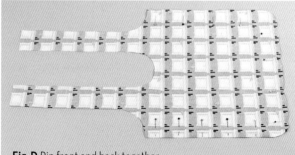

Fig. D Pin front and back together.

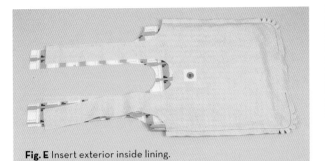

Fig. E Insert exterior inside lining.

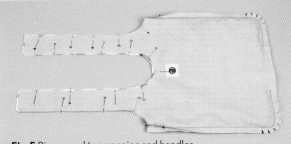

Fig. F Pin around top opening and handles.

ASSEMBLING THE EXTERIOR AND LINING

1. Press the exterior and lining seams open. Turn the exterior right side out. Insert the exterior inside the lining, with right sides together. (**Fig. E**)

2. Pin the exterior and the lining together all around the top opening, including the 4 handles. (**Fig. F**)

3. Sew around the top opening, including across the ends of each of the 4 handles, carefully pivoting at the corners.

4. Trim the corners at the ends of the handles and at the tops of the side seams. Clip the curved seams. (**Fig. G**)

5. Turn the bag right side out through the opening left in the lining. Push out the handle corners. Slipstitch the opening closed. (**Fig. H**)

6. Tuck the lining into the exterior. Press the top opening of the bag, including the handles. (**Fig. I**)

7. Topstitch around the top opening and handles, ⅛″ from the edge. Tie the ends of the handles twice to form a knot. (**Fig. J**)

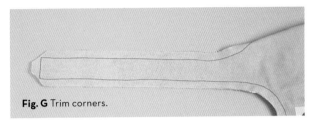

Fig. G Trim corners.

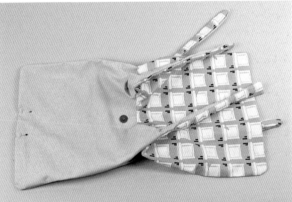

Fig. H Turn right side out. Pin and slipstitch opening closed.

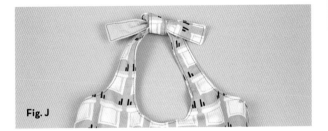

Fig. J

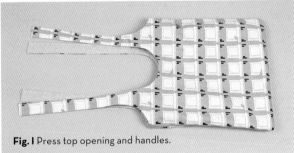

Fig. I Press top opening and handles.

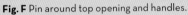

Girl's Bow Headband

Trish Preston

TRISH PRESTON is the designer and owner of Two Peas in a Pod Home-grown Designs, a company offering sewing patterns and professional inspiration. She has appeared on the PBS television show *It's Sew Easy*. Trish offers online courses through her blog. She lives near Columbus, Ohio.

WEBSITE: twopeasinapoddesigns.com

This project originally appeared in *Because I Love You Sew*, by Trish Preston, available from Stash Books.

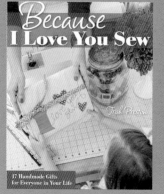

Materials

COTTON: 1 fat quarter (18″ × 22″) for bow

COORDINATING COTTON: 1 fat quarter for ruffle

LACE TRIM: Such as ¾″-wide lace hem tape

FELT: 1 piece 9″ × 12″ in a complementary color

HEADBAND: I love the Goody brand girls' fabric-covered headbands—they are soft to wear.

HOT-GLUE GUN

Cutting

BOW FABRIC

Cut 1 rectangle 3″ × 9″.

Cut 1 square 2½″ × 2½″.

FELT

Cut 1 rectangle 1″ × 4″.

Instructions

Seam allowances are ¼". Follow the instructions for Twice as Nice Bow Tie, Steps 2–6 (page 45), to create the headband bow.

MAKE THE RUFFLE

When making the ruffle, use an unfinished edge for a more vintage look or a finished edge for a more polished look.

For the vintage look:

> Cut 1 rectangle 2" × 12" from the ruffle fabric.

For the more polished look:

> Cut 1 rectangle 3" × 13" from the ruffle fabric.
>
> Press under ¼" along the short edges.
>
> Press under ½" along the long edges.
>
> Stitch around all 4 sides to secure these edges.

PUT IT TOGETHER

1. Stitch a zigzag stitch down the long center of the strip. You can do this by stitching 2 parallel lines of stitching with a slightly longer stitch length. Leave the thread tail ends long, and pull on the bobbin threads only to begin gathering the fabric.

2. Gather the strip evenly until it measures 4".

3. Measure and mark 2" up from one end on the headband.

4. Glue the felt to the underside of the headband with one edge at the 2" mark.

5. Glue the ruffle to the top side of the felt and the headband. Press and hold until the glue cools.

6. Glue the lace trim on the center of the ruffle, covering the gathering stitch.

7. Glue the bow in place.

Photo by Britt Lakin

Lavender Sachet Place Card Tea Bags

Bari J. Ackerman

FINISHED SIZE: 3″ × 3″

Let lavender scent your table by using these tea bag sachets as a fresh take on place cards. Your guest's initial on the tea bag tag personalizes each setting, making it a great party favor. A bowlful makes a lovely centerpiece, too.

BARI J. ACKERMAN is a product and textile designer living in Scottsdale, Arizona. Known for her vintage-inspired accessories and her signature style of mixing fabric prints, Bari has shared her work in many publications, including *Where Women Create* and *Romantic Homes*.

WEBSITE: barijdesigns.com

This project originally appeared in *Inspired to Sew by Bari J.*, by Bari J. Ackerman, available from Stash Books.

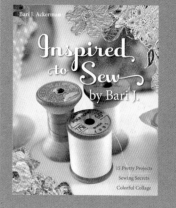

Instructions

MAKE THE TAG

1. Trace the sachet tag pattern A (page 48) on the center of the muslin in pencil or chalk, and write the initial of your choice in the middle of the traced piece.

2. Place the muslin in the embroidery hoop, stretched tight. With the perle cotton, chainstitch the initial. To chainstitch, bring the needle up at 1 and down at the same spot. Looping the thread underneath the needle as shown, bring the needle back up at 2. Insert it in at 2 (inside the loop of the first stitch), and again loop the thread beneath the needle as before, bringing the needle out at 3. Secure the last loop of the chain with a tiny stitch.

3. Press fusible web to the wrong side of an additional piece of muslin slightly larger than the tag.

4. Remove the muslin from the embroidery hoop and layer it on top of the second piece of muslin. Remove the paper from the fusible web and fuse the 2 tag pieces together. Cut out the tag shape, using pinking shears for the bottom edge.

5. Use perle cotton to sew a running stitch about ⅛" from the edges, as shown (at left).

MAKE THE SACHET

1. Fold the piece of printed fabric in half crosswise with right sides together. Press. Sew the side edges together, leaving the top open.

2. At each bottom corner, clip to, but not through, the stitches. Press. Do not turn.

3. To make a box edge on the bottom of the tea bag, stand it straight up and fold a side seam down so the seam and bottom fold are aligned. Using a ¼" seam allowance, sew across the tip of the triangle. Trim off the tip. Repeat for the opposite seam.

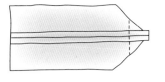

4. Turn the sachet right side out. Fold the side seams in toward the center of the bag and press to create a pleat on each side.

5. Fill the sachet ¾ full of lavender. Trim the top with pinking shears, fold the top down ¼", and press in place. Stitch the sachet closed using a running stitch and perle cotton.

Materials

Makes 1 sachet.

PRINTED FABRIC: 1 piece 6" × 3½" for sachet

DRIED LAVENDER: 2 tablespoons

MUSLIN: 1 piece big enough to fill a small embroidery hoop for tag, plus 1 piece 2" × 3" for tag back

PINKING SHEARS

FELT: Small scrap for leaf

COORDINATING PERLE COTTON EMBROIDERY THREAD

COORDINATING SEWING THREAD

DOUBLE-SIDED FUSIBLE WEB: Such as Wonder-Under

SMALL BUTTON

SMALL EMBROIDERY HOOP

Cutting

FELT: Cut 1 from leaf pattern B (page 48).

EMBELLISH THE SACHET

1. Stitch the vein of the leaf using perle cotton thread and a stem stitch. To sew a stem stitch, bring the needle up at 1 and down at 2, up at 3 and down at 4. Notice that each stitch begins halfway back by the previous stitch.

2. Using the perle cotton thread, sew the button onto the leaf and then onto the sachet. Do not cut the thread.

3. Extend the thread about 6" and sew it to the tag to attach the tag to the bag.

Liberty Bloom Brooch

Alexia Marcelle Abegg

FINISHED SIZE: 3″ diameter

Perfect for your favorite coat or sweater, this simple no-sew flower brooch is a great afternoon project.

Fabric: Blossom-hued Liberty of London print scraps, green print

ALEXIA MARCELLE ABEGG is an award-winning artist and designer who studied fashion and fine arts. She not only designs quilt and sewing patterns, she also teaches, writes, designs fabric for Cotton + Steel, and runs Green Bee Patterns with her mother. Alexia lives in Nashville, Tennessee.

WEBSITE: greenbeepatterns.com

This project originally appeared in *Liberty Love*, by Alexia Marcelle Abegg, available from C&T Publishing.

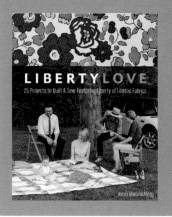

Materials

LIBERTY FABRIC: 1 strip 2½″ × 36″

HEAVYWEIGHT INTERFACING: 1 square 3″ × 3″

FELT: 1 square 3″ × 3″

GREEN PRINT FABRIC: 1 square 3″ × 3″

BAR-STYLE PIN BACK: ¾″ long

GLUE: Fabri-Tac works well.

Cutting

FELT: Cut out a circle 1¾″ in diameter.

HEAVYWEIGHT INTERFACING: Cut out a circle 1½″ in diameter.

Photo by Alexia Abegg

Instructions

PREPARE

1. Use a pea-sized dab of glue to attach a short end of the Liberty strip to the center of the interfacing.

2. Fold the 3″ × 3″ green fabric square as shown to create a leaf. Glue the last fabric fold in place.

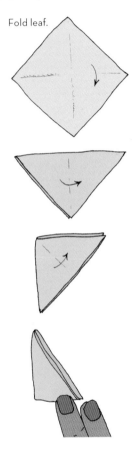

Fold leaf.

3. Let the flower and leaf dry for 1 hour.

ASSEMBLE

1. Wrap and twist the fabric strip around the glued center, placing a tiny bit of glue on the interfacing every so often to anchor the wraps in place.

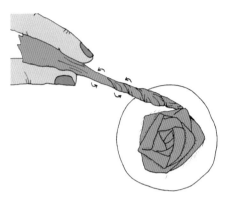

Coil and twist fabric strip into flower shape.

2. Once you have filled the entire interfacing circle, cut the strip, leaving 1″ remaining. Tuck the end around to the back of the interfacing and glue in place.

3. Glue the leaf to the back of the interfacing with the more attractive side faceup.

4. Glue the felt to the back of the interfacing and glue the pin back to the back of the felt.

Let the bloom dry for 24 hours and wear it with your favorite coat, hat, or handbag!

Twice as Nice Bow Tie

Trish Preston

Twins and triplets run in our family, so when my niece had boy/girl twins, it was only natural to come up with a cute way to coordinate their outfits. This sweet little project makes the perfect gift for coordinating siblings—a bow tie for him, and a headband with matching bow tie for her (see Girl's Bow Headband, page 38).

TRISH PRESTON is the designer and owner of Two Peas in a Pod Home-grown Designs, a company offering sewing patterns and professional inspiration. She has appeared on the PBS television show *It's Sew Easy*. Trish offers online courses through her blog. She lives near Columbus, Ohio.

WEBSITE: twopeasinapoddesigns.com

This project originally appeared in *Because I Love You Sew*, by Trish Preston, available from Stash Books.

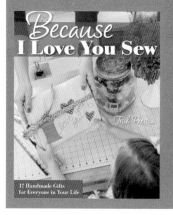

Materials

COTTON: 1 fat quarter (18″ × 22″) for tie

LIGHTWEIGHT FUSIBLE INTERFACING: ¼ yard (such as Shape-Flex)

BOW-TIE HARDWARE: 2 alligator clips or 1 bar-pin back

HOT-GLUE GUN (*optional*)

Cutting

COTTON

Cut 1 rectangle 4″ × 10″.

Cut 1 square 2½″ × 2½″.

INTERFACING

Cut 1 rectangle 4″ × 10″.

Cut 1 square 2½″ × 2½″.

Instructions

Seam allowances are ¼".

1. Following the manufacturer's instructions, fuse the interfacing to the wrong side of the corresponding fabric pieces.

2. Fold the 4" × 10" rectangle in half lengthwise, with rights sides facing, and sew the long side to create a tube. Turn the tube right side out.

tip Use a safety pin to help turn this small tube. Place the pin as shown; then thread it through the tube and gently turn the tube right side out.

3. Center the seam and press. The side with the seam is the back.

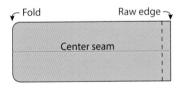

4. With the seam side out, fold the tube in half crosswise and sew the short edges together with a zigzag stitch to create a tube with finished edges. Turn the tube right side out with the new seam at the center back. Set aside.

5. Repeat Steps 2–4 with the 2½" × 2½" square.

6. Pinch the larger tube into an M shape and thread it through the small tube, pulling the small tube to the center of the bow. Tack in place.

7. Attach the hardware to the back of the tie using hot glue or stitch in place. If you're using alligator clips, glue with the teeth facing out so you can clip them to each side of the collar.

Bar-pin back   Two alligator clips

Patterns

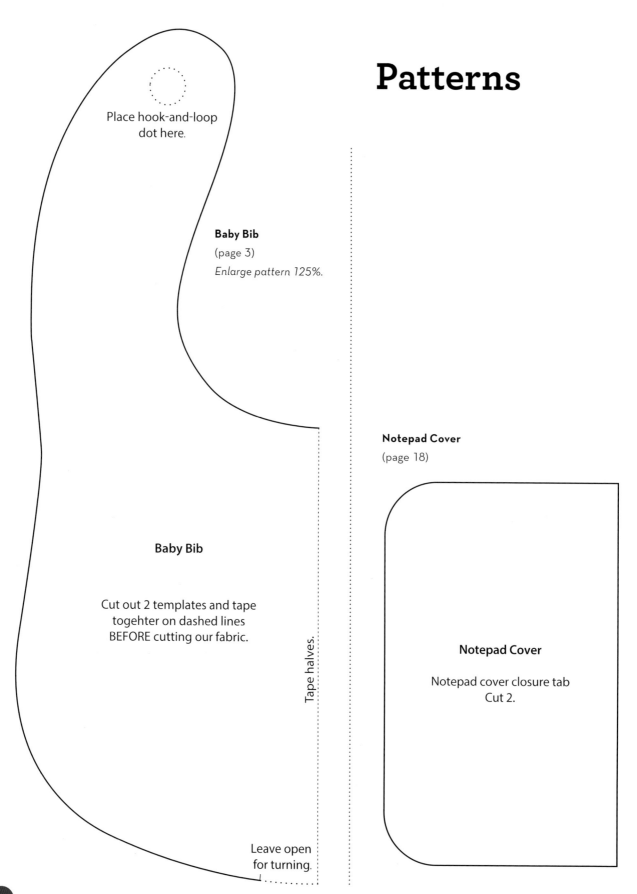

Place hook-and-loop dot here.

Baby Bib
(page 3)
Enlarge pattern 125%.

Baby Bib

Cut out 2 templates and tape togehter on dashed lines BEFORE cutting our fabric.

Tape halves.

Leave open for turning.

Notepad Cover
(page 18)

Notepad Cover

Notepad cover closure tab
Cut 2.

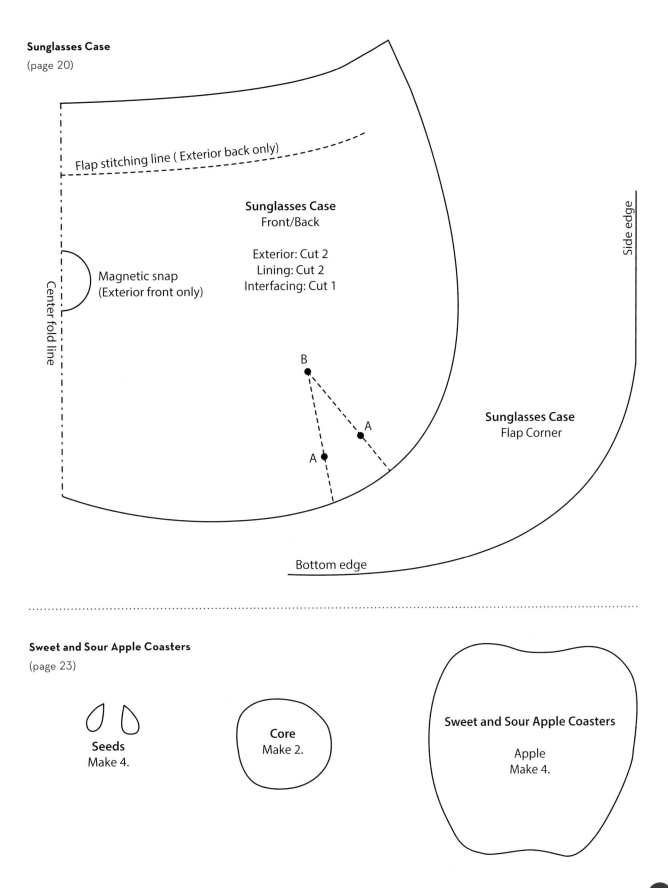

Sunglasses Case

(page 20)

Flap stitching line (Exterior back only)

Sunglasses Case
Front/Back

Exterior: Cut 2
Lining: Cut 2
Interfacing: Cut 1

Magnetic snap
(Exterior front only)

Center fold line

Side edge

B

A

A

Sunglasses Case
Flap Corner

Bottom edge

Sweet and Sour Apple Coasters

(page 23)

Seeds
Make 4.

Core
Make 2.

Sweet and Sour Apple Coasters

Apple
Make 4.

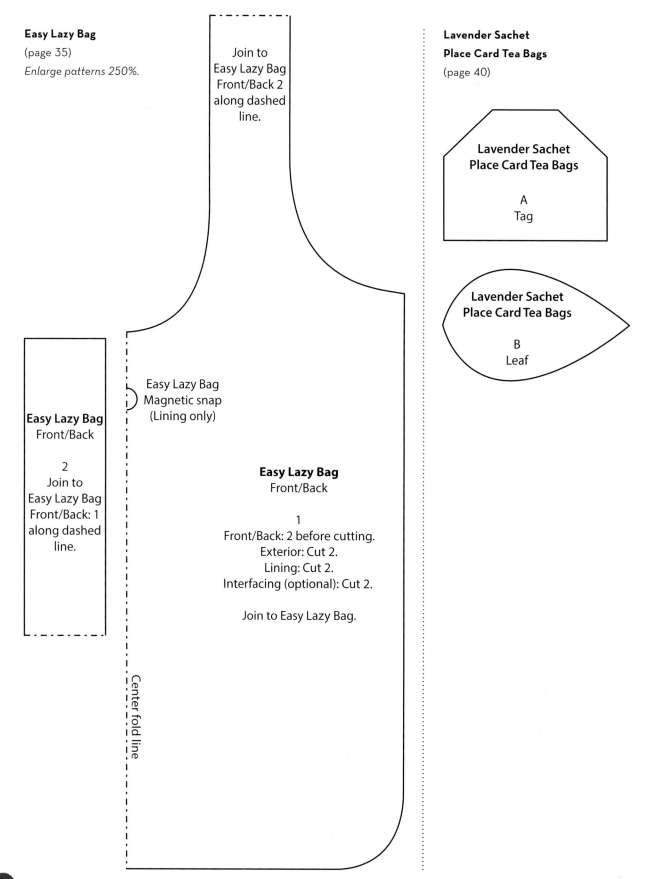

Easy Lazy Bag
(page 35)
Enlarge patterns 250%.

Join to
Easy Lazy Bag
Front/Back 2
along dashed
line.

Lavender Sachet
Place Card Tea Bags
(page 40)

Lavender Sachet
Place Card Tea Bags

A
Tag

Lavender Sachet
Place Card Tea Bags

B
Leaf

Easy Lazy Bag
Magnetic snap
(Lining only)

Easy Lazy Bag
Front/Back

2
Join to
Easy Lazy Bag
Front/Back: 1
along dashed
line.

Easy Lazy Bag
Front/Back

1
Front/Back: 2 before cutting.
Exterior: Cut 2.
Lining: Cut 2.
Interfacing (optional): Cut 2.

Join to Easy Lazy Bag.

Center fold line